A year in Fleurville

Recipes from balconies, rooftops, and gardens

TO SOFIA, CHIARA, AND SIMONE,
AND TO ALL THE CHILDREN WHO SPENT
TOO MUCH TIME INSIDE THEIR HOMES.

THANK YOU TO GÉRALDINE AND FRÉDÉRIC,
WITHOUT WHOM THIS BOOK WOULD NOT
HAVE BEEN MADE.

F.S.

A NOTE ON MEASUREMENTS:
SOMETIMES YOU MAY NOTICE THAT THE NUMBER OF CUPS OR TEASPOONS
I RECOMMEND IN THE INGREDIENTS DOESN'T QUITE MATCH THE
RECOMMENDED WEIGHTS OF THOSE INGREDIENTS. I HAVE KEPT THE
CUP MEASUREMENTS AS SIMPLE AS POSSIBLE FOR A CHILD TO FOLLOW.
THESE RECIPES HAVE ALL BEEN CHOSEN BECAUSE THEY ARE BOUND TO
TURN OUT DELICIOUS, NO MATTER IF YOU ADD A LITTLE MORE OF
SOMETHING, OR A LITTLE LESS.

A year in Fleurville

Recipes from balconies, rooftops, and gardens

Felicita Sala

SCRIBBLE

SPRING HAS ARRIVED IN FLEURVILLE.
AT 10 POMEGRANATE STREET,
EVERYONE IS BUSY IN THE GARDEN:
DIGGING, PLANTING, SOWING,
AND GATHERING.

APRIL

ASPARAGUS STAND
TALL AND STRONG,
LIKE SOLDIERS
GUARDING THE GARDEN.
BUT HERE COMES MARIA
TO CHOP THEM DOWN!

3 SPRING ONIONS, THINLY SLICED

10 FRESH ASPARAGUS, ENDS PEELED AND CHOPPED FINELY

200g GRUYÈRE OR CHEDDAR, GRATED

100g PARMESAN, GRATED

3 EGGS

A PINCH OF SALT

PEPPER

GRATED NUTMEG

125g BUTTER, CUT INTO SMALL CUBES

2 CUPS (250g) FLOUR (half plain, half wholemeal)

½ TSP SALT

1 CUP (250g) HEAVY CREAM OR CRÈME FRAICHE

⅓ CUP (80ml) ICE-COLD WATER

crème

Asparagus Quiche

TO MAKE THE DOUGH, MIX FLOUR, BUTTER, AND ½ TSP SALT WITH YOUR HANDS. ADD WATER AND KNEAD UNTIL SMOOTH. WRAP AND PLACE IN THE FRIDGE FOR HALF AN HOUR. PREHEAT OVEN TO 180°C. FRY THE ASPARAGUS IN A LITTLE OLIVE OIL UNTIL SOFT, KEEPING THE HEADS FOR DECORATION. WHISK TOGETHER THE EGGS, CREAM, NUTMEG, SALT, AND PEPPER. ADD THE SPRING ONIONS, ASPARAGUS, AND GRUYÈRE. ROLL OUT THE DOUGH UNTIL IT'S SLIGHTLY LARGER THAN THE BAKING DISH. PLACE IT ON THE DISH AND PRESS DOWN THE BOTTOM AND SIDES. POKE THE BOTTOM WITH A FORK. POUR FILLING INTO QUICHE BASE. SPRINKLE WITH PARMESAN AND DECORATE WITH ASPARAGUS TOPS. BAKE FOR 45 MINUTES UNTIL GOLDEN ON TOP.

SERVES 6

MAY

ON A BALCONY NEARBY,
MRS THISTLE IS WONDERING
WHAT IT WOULD BE LIKE
TO LIVE INSIDE A GREEN PEA POD,
PERFECTLY ROUND AND COSY AND HAPPY.

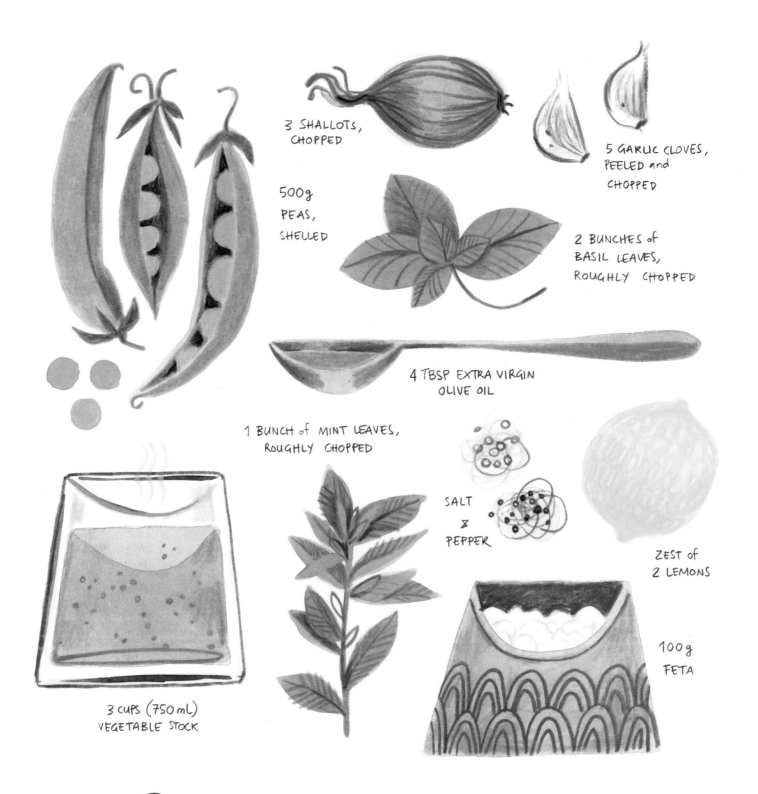

3 SHALLOTS, CHOPPED

5 GARLIC CLOVES, PEELED and CHOPPED

500g PEAS, SHELLED

2 BUNCHES of BASIL LEAVES, ROUGHLY CHOPPED

4 TBSP EXTRA VIRGIN OLIVE OIL

1 BUNCH of MINT LEAVES, ROUGHLY CHOPPED

SALT & PEPPER

ZEST of 2 LEMONS

100g FETA

3 CUPS (750 mL) VEGETABLE STOCK

Pea, Basil, and Mint Soup

IN A LARGE POT, FRY THE SHALLOTS AND GARLIC IN THE OIL UNTIL GOLDEN, STIRRING OFTEN. ADD THE PEAS AND STIR. POUR IN THE STOCK, ADD THE HERBS AND 1 TSP SALT, BRING TO THE BOIL AND COOK FOR 7 MINUTES. BLITZ WITH AN IMMERSION BLENDER UNTIL SMOOTH. MAKE SOME TOAST, RUB A GARLIC CLOVE OVER IT, AND CHOP INTO CROUTONS. PUT THE SOUP IN BOWLS WITH THE CROUTONS, CRUMBLED FETA, LEMON ZEST, A SQUEEZE OF LEMON JUICE, PEPPER, AND A SPRINKLE OF OLIVE OIL.

SERVES 6-8

JUNE

A TREE IS READY TO BE PICKED
ON TAMARIND AVENUE.
SOME CHERRIES ARE USED AS EARRINGS,
SOME AS AMMUNITION,
AND SOME ARE GATHERED
FOR A SPECIAL TREAT.

½ CUP (80g)
PLAIN FLOUR

6 TBSP (60g)
SUGAR

2 CUPS CHERRIES,
PITTED

2 EGGS + 1 YOLK

A PINCH
OF SALT

¾ CUP (200ml)
MILK

1 TSP
VANILLA
EXTRACT

2 TBSP (25g)
BUTTER

Cherry Clafoutis

PREHEAT THE OVEN TO 180°C. CHOP THE CHERRIES IN HALF AND SPRINKLE WITH 1 TBSP SUGAR. GREASE A PIE DISH WITH BUTTER AND SPRINKLE WITH SUGAR. PLACE THE CHERRIES IN THE DISH AND BAKE FOR 5 MINUTES TO SOFTEN THEM. MELT THE BUTTER GENTLY IN A SMALL PAN AND SET ASIDE. IN A BOWL, WHISK THE EGGS, 5 TBSP SUGAR, AND VANILLA. ADD FLOUR, AND PINCH OF SALT, AND WHISK UNTIL SMOOTH. ADD MILK AND BUTTER. MIX WELL. POUR THE BATTER INTO THE PIE DISH OVER THE CHERRIES AND SERVE WARM WITH A SCOOP OF VANILLA ICE CREAM.

SERVES 6-8

JULY

JUST OUTSIDE THE CITY, CUCUMBERS
HAVE SLOWLY CREPT UP A TRELLIS.
THEY ARE COOL AND CRISP;
TORPEDOES FULL OF WATER ON HOT DAYS.
RAMON IS ABOUT TO FIND OUT
IF THEY CAN FLOAT.

½ TSP GROUND CUMIN

1 SMALL CUCUMBER

1½ CUPS FULL-FAT GREEK YOGHURT

2 TBSP EXTRA VIRGIN OLIVE OIL

1 TBSP LEMON JUICE

1 GARLIC CLOVE, MASHED TO A PASTE

1 TBSP FRESH DILL, MINCED

1 TSP HONEY

SALT

Tzatziki

GRATE THE CUCUMBER, SPRINKLE WITH A PINCH OF SALT, AND SQUEEZE THE WATER OUT THROUGH A SIEVE OR A CLEAN CLOTH. COMBINE YOGHURT, GARLIC, OIL, HONEY, CUMIN, LEMON, AND ½ TSP SALT, AND LET IT REST IN THE FRIDGE FOR A COUPLE OF HOURS. ADD CUCUMBER AND DILL, AND MIX WELL. SERVE WITH TOASTED FLATBREAD.

MAKES 2 CUPS.

AUGUST

UP HIGH, CLOSE TO THE SKY, THE SUMMER SUN
MAKES PEPPERS TURN DIFFERENT COLOURS,
LIKE TRAFFIC LIGHTS. INSIDE THEY ARE HOLLOW,
SO THERE IS LOTS OF SPACE TO PUT OTHER THINGS.

2 PEPPERS, HALVED AND DESEEDED

1 BUNCH OF PARSLEY, MINCED

4 TBSP EXTRA VIRGIN OLIVE OIL

3 TSP CAPERS IN VINEGAR

1 TOMATO OR 3 SUNDRIED TOMATOES, OR BOTH

8 ANCHOVY FILLETS

1 GARLIC CLOVE

SALT AND PEPPER

2 CUPS DAY-OLD BREAD, CRUSTS REMOVED AND CUT INTO CHUNKS

Stuffed Peppers

PREHEAT OVEN TO 180°C. ROUGHLY CHOP THE TOMATOES AND CAPERS, AND MINCE THE GARLIC. IN A BOWL, MIX THE BREAD CHUNKS WITH TOMATOES, CAPERS, GARLIC, ANCHOVIES, PARSLEY, AND OLIVE OIL. ADD ½ TSP SALT. LINE AN OVEN TRAY WITH BAKING PAPER, DRIZZLE WITH OLIVE OIL, AND ADD A PINCH OF SALT AND 2 TBSP WATER. FILL THE PEPPER HALVES WITH THE MIX AND PLACE ON TRAY. DRIZZLE GENEROUSLY WITH OLIVE OIL AND BAKE FOR 40-45 MINUTES. SERVE WITH ROAST POTATOES.

SERVES 4

SEPTEMBER

LIKE GREEN AND YELLOW LANTERNS,
PEARS FILL A TREE ON PUMPERNICKEL LANE.
AND NOW THEY'VE FOUND THEIR WAY INSIDE A KITCHEN
TO BE CHOPPED, GRATED, BITTEN, AND SWALLOWED.
THEY ARE JUICY AND PURE.

2 FIRM PEARS, GRATED

A PINCH OF SALT

3 TBSP SUGAR

1 CUP RICOTTA

SPLASH OF LEMON JUICE

2 CUPS (275g) FLOUR

2 EGGS

½ CUP MILK

2 TSP BAKING POWDER

Pear and Ricotta Pancakes

MASH THE RICOTTA WITH THE SUGAR. ADD THE EGGS AND BEAT UNTIL SMOOTH. ADD THE GRATED PEARS, MILK, SALT, AND LEMON JUICE, AND STIR. ADD THE FLOUR AND BAKING POWDER GRADUALLY, AND MIX WELL. LET THE MIXTURE SIT IN THE FRIDGE FOR 1 HOUR. IF THE BATTER IS TOO THICK, ADD A LITTLE MILK AND STIR. POUR 2-3 TBSP OF BATTER ON TO A HOT PAN WITH SOME BUTTER. TURN EACH PANCAKE AFTER IT STARTS TO FORM BUBBLES, AND FINISH COOKING ON THE OTHER SIDE FOR ABOUT 30 SECONDS. SERVE WITH HONEY AND LEMON OR MAPLE SYRUP.

MAKES 12

OCTOBER

IN THIS NEIGHBOURHOOD,
MANY SEEDS WERE PLANTED BY MANY HANDS.
IN THEIR PLACE THERE ARE NOW SQUASHES.
THEY SIT ON THE GROUND WITH THEIR HEAVY BOTTOMS,
WAITING TO BE TRANSFORMED INTO CAKES,
SOUPS, OR SCARY FACES.

1 KG BUTTERNUT SQUASH, PEELED AND CUBED

½ CUP (100g) SOFT BROWN SUGAR

2 TBSP FINE BREADCRUMBS

A PINCH OF SALT

3 EGGS, BEATEN

2 TBSP (30g) MELTED BUTTER

1 CUP (100g) ALMOND FLOUR

2 CUPS (500ml) WHOLE MILK

1 TSP CINNAMON

ICING SUGAR

A HANDFUL OF SLICED ALMONDS

Butternut Cake

SIMMER SQUASH IN MILK OVER LOW HEAT FOR 30 MINUTES UNTIL SOFT. DRAIN IN A COLANDER AND LEAVE TO COOL, SQUEEZING OUT EXCESS LIQUID. IN A BOWL, BEAT THE EGGS WITH SUGAR, BUTTER, ALMOND FLOUR, BREADCRUMBS, CINNAMON, AND SALT. STIR IN THE SQUASH UNTIL SMOOTH. POUR INTO A GREASED PIE DISH, SPRINKLE ALMONDS ON TOP, AND BAKE IN THE OVEN AT 180°C FOR 45-50 MINUTES UNTIL GOLDEN. WHEN THE CAKE HAS COOLED DOWN, SPRINKLE WITH ICING SUGAR.

SERVES 8-10

NOVEMBER

IN A FANCY GARDEN
IN THE CITY CENTRE,
THE EARTH IS HIDING
SOMETHING BRIGHT.
HERE ARE THE BEETROOTS
UNDER GIANT GREEN UMBRELLAS.
SOPHIE PULLS ONE OUT;
A DEEP-PURPLE TROPHY!

3 MEDIUM BEETROOTS

1 GARLIC CLOVE, MINCED

2 TBSP TAHINI

3 TBSP FULL-FAT GREEK YOGHURT

1 TBSP EXTRA VIRGIN OLIVE OIL

SPLASH OF LEMON JUICE

SALT

A HANDFUL OF TOASTED PINE NUTS

Roasted Beet Dip

PREHEAT OVEN TO 180°C. PUT BEETROOTS IN A SMALL ROASTING PAN WITH HALF A GLASS OF WATER. COVER WITH FOIL AND BAKE FOR 1 HOUR. LET THE BEETS COOL AND THEN PEEL THEM, CUT THEM INTO CHUNKS, AND PUREE WITH AN IMMERSION BLENDER, ALONG WITH THE GARLIC. ADD OLIVE OIL, YOGHURT, TAHINI, LEMON JUICE, AND SALT TO TASTE. POUR INTO A BOWL AND SPRINKLE WITH TOASTED PINE NUTS. SERVE WITH TOASTED BREAD.

MAKES 1½ CUPS

DECEMBER

POTATOES ARE STORED
FOR THE WINTER
IN FATIMA'S CELLAR.
THEY LOVE DARK, COOL PLACES.
IT REMINDS THEM OF
WHEN THEY WERE BABIES,
DEEP INSIDE THE EARTH.

2 MEDIUM POTATOES
(APPROX. 250g),
PEELED AND CHOPPED

2 TBSP GRATED PARMESAN

1 CUP MILK
+2 CUPS WATER

2 BAY
LEAVES

1 EGG

300g
COD FILLET
OR OTHER WHITE FISH

1 GARLIC CLOVE,
MINCED

LEMON
ZEST

A HANDFUL
OF PARSLEY,
FINELY CHOPPED

3 TBSP BREADCRUMBS

SALT AND
PEPPER

VEGETABLE
OIL

Potato and Cod Croquettes

PUT THE FISH IN A SAUCEPAN AND COVER WITH MILK AND WATER. ADD BAY LEAVES AND BRING
TO A BOIL. COOK FOR 4 MINUTES AND TAKE OUT THE FISH WITH A SLOTTED SPOON. LEAVE IT TO COOL,
THEN CRUMBLE IT WITH A FORK AND TAKE OUT ANY BONES. ADD POTATOES TO THE SAME SAUCEPAN
AND COOK UNTIL SOFT. DRAIN THE POTATOES AND PLACE THEM IN A BOWL WITH THE COD. MASH
WITH A BIG PINCH OF SALT, THEN MIX IN THE EGG, PARMESAN, PARSLEY, PEPPER, GARLIC, AND
A LITTLE LEMON ZEST. MIX WELL UNTIL SMOOTH AND THEN FORM INTO CYLINDERS. COAT THE
FISHCAKES IN BREADCRUMBS IN A SHALLOW DISH. HEAT SOME OIL IN A PAN. FRY THE CAKES
FOR 3 MINUTES ON EACH SIDE UNTIL GOLDEN BROWN. DRAIN, SPRINKLE WITH SALT, AND SERVE WITH
A SPLASH OF LEMON JUICE AND A DOLLOP OF MAYONNAISE. MAKES 18

JANUARY

ON A TREE ON A BALCONY ON CAULIFLOWER ROAD,
TINY LEMON SUNS BRIGHTEN A DARK WINTER DAY.
A ROSEMARY BUSH GROWS HERE TOO.
THEY KEEP EACH OTHER COMPANY AND ARE VERY GOOD FRIENDS.

ZEST OF
2 LEMONS

JUICE OF
1 LEMON

4 GARLIC
CLOVES

1 CUP (200g) DRY CANNELLINI BEANS
(MAKES 400g COOKED BEANS, DRAINED)

EXTRA VIRGIN
OLIVE OIL

2 SPRIGS OF FRESH
ROSEMARY

1 CUP BEAN-
COOKING LIQUID

olive oi

SALT

PEPPER

Lemony Bean Dip

SOAK THE BEANS IN WATER OVERNIGHT. DRAIN THE BEANS AND COOK IN A POT OF WATER
WITH 1 CLOVE OF GARLIC AND 1 SPRIG OF ROSEMARY FOR 1 HOUR UNTIL SOFT. ADD 1 TSP
SALT AT THE END AND LET THEM REST, THEN DRAIN THE BEANS AND KEEP 1 CUP OF LIQUID.
FINELY CHOP 3 CLOVES OF GARLIC AND THE LEAVES FROM A SPRIG OF ROSEMARY AND GENTLY
FRY IN OLIVE OIL FOR 2 MINUTES, STIRRING. ADD THE WARM, GARLICKY OIL TO A BOWL
WITH THE BEANS AND A FEW TABLESPOONS OF BEAN-COOKING LIQUID. SQUASH THE MIX
WITH A FORK OR PUREE WITH A BLENDER. ADD THE LEMON JUICE, THE ZEST, SALT AND
PEPPER, AND MIX. PLACE IN A BOWL AND DRIZZLE WITH 3 TBSP EXTRA VIRGIN OLIVE OIL.
SERVE WITH FRESH BREAD.

MAKES 2 CUPS.

FEBRUARY

HOW LUCKY TO HAVE AN ORANGE TREE RIGHT BEHIND YOUR HOUSE!
JUICY PLANETS HANG LIKE GIFTS FOR THE CHILDREN OF CINNAMON STREET.
BABY LEO TRIES TO BITE ONE WITH ONLY TWO TEETH, AND FAILS.

3/4 CUP (180 ml)
EXTRA VIRGIN
OLIVE OIL

JUICE AND ZEST OF
2 BLOOD ORANGES
(ABOUT 200ml OF JUICE)

1 CUP (200g)
SUGAR

3 EGGS

½ CUP (120 ml)
PLAIN YOGHURT
OR MILK

2 CUPS
(275g)
PLAIN
FLOUR

1 TSP
BAKING POWDER

A PINCH
OF SALT

Blood Orange and Olive Oil Cake

PREHEAT THE OVEN TO 180°C. BUTTER AND FLOUR A 20-23 cm CAKE TIN. RUB SUGAR AND ORANGE ZEST TOGETHER IN A BOWL. WHISK IN THE EGGS ONE BY ONE. ADD THE YOGHURT OR MILK, OLIVE OIL, AND ORANGE JUICE. ADD THE FLOUR, SALT, AND BAKING POWDER, AND MIX WELL. POUR INTO CAKE TIN AND BAKE FOR ABOUT 45 MINUTES, UNTIL A SKEWER COMES OUT CLEAN. LET COOL AND SPRINKLE WITH ICING SUGAR.

SERVES 8

MARCH

A HERB FOREST
GROWS INSIDE THIS HOME.
SAMUEL WISHES HE COULD GO
CAMPING IN A REAL FOREST.
'SOON,' SAYS GRANDPA.
'WHEN THE RAIN SEASON STOPS.'

250g DRY CHICKPEAS

CORIANDER

PARSLEY

DILL

EXTRA VIRGIN OLIVE OIL

1 GARLIC CLOVE, MINCED

1 SMALL BUNCH EACH, CHOPPED

MINT

1 TBSP FLOUR + ½ TSP BAKING POWDER

½ RED ONION, FINELY CHOPPED

1 TSP GROUND CUMIN

½ TSP GROUND CORIANDER SEEDS

ZEST OF 1 LEMON

1 TSP SALT

VEGETABLE OIL

½ CUP TAHINI

JUICE OF 1 LEMON

PEPPER

½ TSP BAKING SODA

½ TSP SMOKED PAPRIKA

Herb Felafels with Tahini Sauce

SOAK THE CHICKPEAS OVERNIGHT WITH ½ TSP BAKING SODA. COMBINE THE DRAINED CHICKPEAS IN A MIXER WITH THE GARLIC, ONION, HERBS, AND SPICES. BLITZ UNTIL FINELY GROUND, THEN PLACE IN A BOWL WITH SALT AND PEPPER, FLOUR MIXED WITH BAKING POWDER, A DRIZZLE OF OLIVE OIL, AND THE LEMON ZEST. MIX WELL AND SHAPE INTO ROUND BALLS USING ABOUT 2 TSP OF THE MIXTURE, THEN FLATTEN THEM A LITTLE. HEAT THE VEGETABLE OIL IN A DEEP POT AND FRY THE FELAFELS IN BATCHES FOR 1-2 MINUTES ON EACH SIDE UNTIL GOLDEN BROWN. TO MAKE THE SAUCE, WHISK THE LEMON JUICE AND TAHINI TOGETHER WITH A BIG PINCH OF SALT AND PAPRIKA. AS IT BECOMES THICK, ADD WATER LITTLE BY LITTLE, AND WHISK UNTIL SMOOTH AND CREAMY. SERVE FELAFELS WITH TAHINI SAUCE AND A GREEN SALAD.

MAKES 18-20 FELAFELS

THERE ARE WINTER DAYS WHEN IT SEEMS
THE WHOLE WORLD IS ASLEEP.
SEEDS REST INSIDE THE EARTH,
AND EVEN THE TREES SEEM TO BE WAITING.

THEN ONE DAY, TINY PINK FLOWERS
EMERGE FROM WHO - KNOWS - WHERE.

AND JUST LIKE THE FLOWERS,
PEOPLE COME OUT OF THEIR HOMES AGAIN.
FROM ALL OVER THE CITY THEY GATHER TOGETHER
FOR THE BIGGEST PICNIC OF THE YEAR.

MUSIC AND BLANKETS
AND BASKETS FULL OF FOOD —
SPRING HAS RETURNED TO FLEURVILLE!

GARDENING ACTIONS

8 ⬬ | 16

SOWING:

THE BIGGER THE SEED, THE DEEPER IT MUST GO:
IT SHOULD BE BURIED TO A DEPTH ABOUT
TWICE ITS SIZE.

TRANSPLANTING:

ONCE A PLANT HAS GROWN A LITTLE,
MOVE IT TO A BIGGER POT OR TO THE
GROUND SO ITS ROOTS CAN EXPAND.

WATERING:

PLANTS DON'T NEED TOO MUCH
WATER. WATER IN THE MORNING
OR AT NIGHT, TO KEEP MOISTURE IN.

PEEING IN YOUR
WATERING CAN
HELPS THE SOIL!

MIXING:

MORE VARIETY IN YOUR GARDEN MEANS PLANTS
GET LESS SICK. PLANT VEGETABLES TOGETHER
WITH AROMATIC HERBS AND FLOWERS.
THIS WILL ATTRACT BEES AND INSECTS,
WHO WILL HELP YOUR FRUIT AND
VEGETABLES TO GROW!

MULCHING:
BY COVERING THE EARTH WITH STRAW, LEAVES, DRY GRASS, OR WOOD CHIPS, YOU WILL PROTECT THE SOIL, WATER LESS, AND STOP WEEDS FROM GROWING.

CARING FOR THE SOIL:
AVOID CHEMICAL FERTILISERS. MANY THINGS FOUND IN NATURE CAN ENRICH YOUR SOIL, SUCH AS COMPOST, WHICH YOU CAN MAKE FROM FOOD SCRAPS.

RECYCLING:
THERE ARE LOTS OF THINGS YOU CAN RE-USE IN YOUR GARDEN: PAPER AND FOOD SCRAPS FOR COMPOST, JARS AND CANS FOR SEEDLINGS, COOKING WATER FOR WATERING, AND SEEDS FOR PLANTING.

HARVESTING:
PICKING YOUR FRUIT AND VEG IS THE BEST PART OF GARDENING. TIME TO COOK AND SHARE YOUR FOOD!

SHARING:
EXCHANGING PLANTS, SEEDS, AND PRODUCE — AS WELL AS KNOWLEDGE AND OBSERVATIONS — IS A GREAT WAY TO ENRICH YOUR GARDEN AND HELP SOMEONE ELSE DO THE SAME.

SEEDS

YOU CAN SAVE YOUR OWN FRUIT AND VEGETABLE SEEDS
AND SHARE OR SWAP THEM WITH FRIENDS.

TOMATO

PARSLEY

CORN

BEETROOT

PEPPER

SQUASH

COURGETTE

ASPARAGUS

PEACH

AVOCADO

WHEAT

SUNFLOWER

PEAR

CHERRY

LEMON

OAT

CARROT

POTATO

WATERMELON

POMEGRANATE

SESAME

BROCCOLI

CHEVRIL

BEANS,
LENTILS,
PEAS

CUCUMBER

GARDENING TOOLS

HERE ARE SOME THINGS YOU CAN USE TO START YOUR OWN VEGETABLE GARDEN. YOU CAN USE TOOLS FROM YOUR HOUSE TOO, LIKE A FORK!

POTS

GOOD SOIL

CULTIVATOR

GARDEN TROWEL

FORK

SPADE

RAISED GARDEN BED

GARDENING GLOVES

WATERING CAN

WELLINGTON BOOTS

SECATEURS

FRUIT + VEGETABLES

IT'S GOOD FOR YOU AND GOOD FOR THE EARTH WHEN YOU EAT FRUIT AND VEG THAT ARE IN SEASON. HERE ARE A FEW EXAMPLES:

SWISS CHARD

BROAD BEANS

ARTICHOKE

ASPARAGUS

TURNIP

PEAS

SPINACH

STRAWBERRY

LETTUCE

SPRING ONION

RADICCHIO

Spring

ROSEMARY

THYME

OREGANO

SAGE

DILL

HERBS: ALL YEAR

COURGETTE

GREEN BEANS

CHERRY

BERRIES

Summer

CUCUMBER

PEACH

MELONS

AUBERGINE

PLUM

PEPPER

TOMATO

KALE

CHICORY

CABBAGE

KIWI

JERUSALEM ARTICHOKE

CAULIFLOWER

BROCCOLI

DAIKON

PARSLEY

Winter

MINT

BAY LEAF

BASIL

CITRUS FRUIT

LEEK

POTATO

MUSHROOMS

FIG

POMEGRANATE

Autumn

APPLE

GRAPES

SQUASH

CARROT

BEETROOT

FENNEL

PEAR

CHESTNUT